Historical Information	2.
Barrowford to Barley 3.2 miles	6.
Barley to Rigg of England 3.7 miles	8.
Rigg of England to Higham 2 miles	10.
Higham to Law Farm 3.6 miless	12.
Law Farm to Read Old Bridge 2 miles	14.
Read Old Bridge to Clitheroe 4.9 miles	16.
Clitheroe to Hancocks Farm 3.0 miles	18.
Hancocks Farm to Fell Side 3.7 miles	20.
Fell Side to Slaidburn 2.1 miles	22.
Slaidburn to Lanshaw 1.3 miles	22.
Lanshaw to High Salter 8.6 miles	24.
High Salter to Deep Clough 2.3 miles	26.
Deep Clough to Crook O'Lune 5.7 miles	28.
Crook O'Lune to Lancaster Castle 4.9 miles	30.
Acknowledgements	32.

Some history of the Lancashire Witches, and its walk
- A wonderful and complex story of Prejudice:

This introductory article only touches on a few highlights of the relevant matter. For a much more balanced and detailed view of the history, read and enjoy John Clayton's excellent *The Pendle Witch Fourth Centenary Handbook*. John has written several books on the topic, was consultant to the BBC4 TV programme on the subject, and is acknowledged as the primary academic on the Witches. There was also a rash of Victorian "romantic" novels around the story, some of which achieved such popularity that their tales were and are often accepted as fact. Also, beware; many of the accused had multiple surnames.

James 1st inherited continual conflict between Protestants and Catholics, which dogged him throughout his reigns in Scotland and England. He also became somewhat obsessed with witchcraft. On his return from Denmark with his new wife Anne (also reputed to have flirted with Catholicism) he blamed the stormy weather on the North Berwick Witches, and wrote a book on the subject, (called *Daemonologie*, which made a case for suspending the normal rules of evidence for witchcraft trials), subsequently used to "prove" the Lancashire accused were witches. Following the Gunpowder plot in 1605 he became even more sensitised. Not all he did was by any means negative. For example: He authorised the well-liked King James Bible; and created the role of Sovereign's Poet Laureate, which post has survived to this day.

In this part of Lancashire, following the Pilgrimage of Grace, the break-up of the Abbeys created significant growth of "nouveau riche" landowners, anxious to prove their support for the monarchy. Yet many of the "lower orders" had a deep and abiding preference for the old religion. This created a fertile seed-bed for the events we are interested in. For the Magistrates and Justices, prosecuting "witches", plus a whiff of Catholicism, was an effective way to curry favour at James's court. The events were also very probably: anti-folk medicine, probably urged by the then-emerging "orthodox" medical professions; anti-rural, from the then urban elite; and anti-northern, from a London-based Clerk of the Court (Liverpool-born) and the Justices.

Witches were almost all women, so the prosecution also appears blatantly anti-feminine. Witches scraped a meagre living, typically offering: physical medicine, using herbal, poultice and similar treatments; bone-setting; and midwifery, on humans and animals; as well as attempting psychological help, via spells and curses. They were typically single parents, trying to survive on the edges of society, advertising their services via vivid attention-getting stories, which spread rapidly by word of mouth. In this case, those stories backfired badly.

Demdike's (Elizabeth Southern's) granddaughter, Alizon Device, met a pedlar, James Law, from Halifax, asking him for some pins. Law refused such a small transaction, stumbled and fell, perhaps a stroke, later dying. She reportedly confessed and asked for his son's forgiveness. She, her mother Elizabeth Device, and brother, James, were summoned to appear before the magistrate, Roger Nowell, of Read Hall, on 30th March 1612. Alizon confessed she had told the Devil to lame Law, after he had called her a thief. Her brother said his sister had bewitched a local child. Elizabeth admitted that her mother, Demdike, had a mark on her body, regarded as left by the Devil after he had sucked her blood. When questioned about Anne Whittle (Chattox), Alizon perhaps saw an opportunity for revenge.

On 2nd April 1612, Demdike, Chattox, and Chattox's daughter Anne Redferne, were summoned before Nowell. Demdike and Chattox were blind and in their eighties. Both apparently provided Nowell with confessions. Anne Redferne made no confession. Based on the evidence and confessions he had obtained, Nowell committed Demdike, Chattox, Anne Redferne and Alizon Device to Lancaster assizes.

Committal and subsequent trial of the four women might have been the end of the matter but for a meeting, organised by Elizabeth Device at Malkin Tower, on 6th April 1612, Good Friday. To feed the party, James Device stole a neighbour's sheep. When word reached Roger Nowell, he investigated. On 27th April 1612, Nowell and another magistrate, Nicholas Bannister, examined the events at Malkin Tower, asking who attended and what had happened there. Eight more people were accused of witchcraft and committed for trial: Elizabeth Device, James Device, Alice Nutter, Katherine Hewitt, John Bulcock, Jane Bulcock, Alice Gray and Jennet Preston were sent to Lancaster Gaol, to join the four already there. The so-called "coven" at Malkin Tower was possibly a Catholic Mass, but saying this would have inflicted on all those present accusations of "recusancy", penalties for which were almost as bad as those for witchcraft.

In total, twenty "local" "witches" were arrested. In those days the hearings were infrequent, then quick, and mostly used the written evidence extracted by the Magistrates. Jennet Preston, from Gisburn, was sent to York for trial, and found guilty at the second attempt, on 27th July 1612, before the same Justices who later held this Lancaster trial, probably creating a major supposition in those Justices' minds. Another, Elizabeth Southern, died while held awaiting trial. Three, Jane Southworth, Jennet Brierley, and Ellen Brierley, from another unconnected case at Salmesbury, were acquitted quite quickly, on 18th August 1612. One, Isobel Robey, from near to St Helens, was included in the "job lot", for unconnected reasons. However, nine-year-old Jennet Device was a key witness for the prosecution. The rest had been persuaded to turn on each other, between the two key families involved (Demdike and Chattox), along with a great deal of chicanery by the Magistrates, and manoeuvring between the accused and those giving evidence. Their trials were held on the 18th and 19th August 1612, again in front of Sir James Altham and Sir Edward Bromley. As a result, nine of the remainder were hung at Lancaster, along with the St Helens lady, on 20th August, 1612, and one (Alice Gray) acquitted.

Jennet Device's influence went far beyond Lancashire. Thomas Potts' writings and Jennet's evidence were included in a reference handbook for magistrates, *The Country Justice*. It began use by all magistrates, including those in the colonies, such as America, and led them to seek the testimony of children in trials of witchcraft. So, at the notorious Salem witch trials in 1692, most of the evidence was given by children. Nineteen more people were hanged.

Thomas Potts later wrote *The Wonderfull Discoverie of Witches in the Countie of Lancaster*, which was really aimed at getting him and the Justices preferment at James's Court. That ploy was moderately successful. There is now a new edition of the book, modernised to readability and introduced by Robert Poole.

The walk route was aimed at being completely legal, relevantly accurate and a worthwhile walk. John Clayton's book was used to identify as many of the key locations around Pendle Water as were feasible to visit. These are used, avoiding main roads as much as possible, through to Read Hall. However, after the prisoners left Ashlar House (where they were "examined") and Read Hall, we have no specific evidence of their journey. It was normal for the Constable (Henry Hargreaves) to be given a lump-sum fee for organising such transport, so there was no reason for detailed records. It is probable that they were carried in a cart, as Chattox and Demdike were very unlikely to be able to walk. Normal practice was to take such accused though the key population centres and put them in the stocks, to allow the local populace to express their opinions at stops along the way. We have assumed Clitheroe and Slaidburn as the only likely candidates for this. That suggests two possible key routes onward: either Trough Road, leading NW from Newton; or the Roman/Salter Fell Road, leading NW from Slaidburn. A short look at the Trough Road from across the valley shows it to have been built from massive quantities of tipped stone, unfeasible before at least the late 18thC. By definition, the Roman Road did exist, so the Salter Fell route was chosen and is also a far better walk. Legal footpaths from then on are difficult in the Lancaster area, so we filtered down to and along the Lune Valley Ramble, then the recently legalised Grimshaw Lane, through the neighbourhood of Gallows Hill (shown as Tyburn on old maps), then back up the route we know the witches followed from the prison, to be hung. It's also worth getting a tour of Lancaster Castle, including the relevant dungeons – see http://www.lancastercastle.com/home.php

We hope you enjoy walking it, and the history, as much as we do.

Barrowford To Barley 3.2 Miles

Start. At the car park opposite the Pendle Heritage Centre in Barrowford SD862307 (if leaving a vehicle, please leave a voluntary donation in the honesty box in the west corner). Leave the car park by the small gate in the northwest corner. Through the gate and follow the enclosed paths, with Pendle Water on your left, to exit near a road bridge. Turn right and cross Higherford Road with care, going down Pinfold. After 50m, turn sharp left down Calder View to reach a cobbled path and cross the bridge over Pendle Water. Turn left for another 50m, turning right at Brook Dell House, into an enclosed path.

2. Ascend through a wooded area to reach a stile leading to open fields. Head diagonally north-west across the field to pass between trees, then turn half left to head west across an open field to reach a stile. Now continue in the same direction to reach a gate and gain access to a farm track.

3. Over the track and cross a stile ahead and drop down to cross a footbridge over a stream. Go ahead, with a fence on your right, to cross a stile. Turn right on the surfaced track. After 50m, turn left off the track to cross a stile and shortly turn right over a footbridge. Now, with a hedge on the right, head uphill to cross a stile next to a farm building. Follow the track, uphill, for about 400m, with a field boundary on your left. Cross a stone stile at the top of the hill.

4. Head downhill and west over open ground, passing a lone tree, to a signpost. Turn left at the post and down to cross the stepping stones over the stream. (If the stream is in flood there are paths and stream crossings northeast and south west of the stepping stones.)

5. Go up the bank, to cross the stile into the road, and go forward on the minor road to the metal field gate ahead. Through the gate into the field and ahead bearing left through another gate and on, to follow a fingerpost. Over a stile at the field corner. Now follow the hedge on your right to another stile and cross another field to cross a stile near the static home park and turn right into a lane. Follow this for 100m to a turn left though a kissing-gate.

6. Cross three fields (stiles and gates) to SD838403. Cross the stile here and turn left. Follow the field edge downhill to reach a field track. Turn right on the track and through several gates to reach a farm access track. Turn left on the track to reach a road. Turn right on the road, with river and white fence on the left, to reach a road bridge. Over the bridge and immediate right through a gap in the fence. Now follow the riverside path in a north-westerly direction for 0.4 miles to reach the road at Whitehough Outdoor Education Centre.

7. Cross the bridge and turn left, with the river on your left, and follow it past the building and houses for 150m to a stone stile in the wall on the right. Head uphill to the woodland edge, passing through a kissing gate, to another gate leading into a field. Head diagonally left in a westerly direction to a kissing gate at the top edge of the plantation. Through this gate and into open ground heading slightly uphill to a stile in the top far corner.

8. Through the stile and now gently downhill to pass the isolated building on your left, then across the slope and through a tight stile to the right of a metal gate. After a short distance go through a stile on your left, in a rough scrubby area, and follow the path, with the wall on the right, downhill to a riverside path in Barley Village. Head north on Barley Lane until the old chapel is on your right.

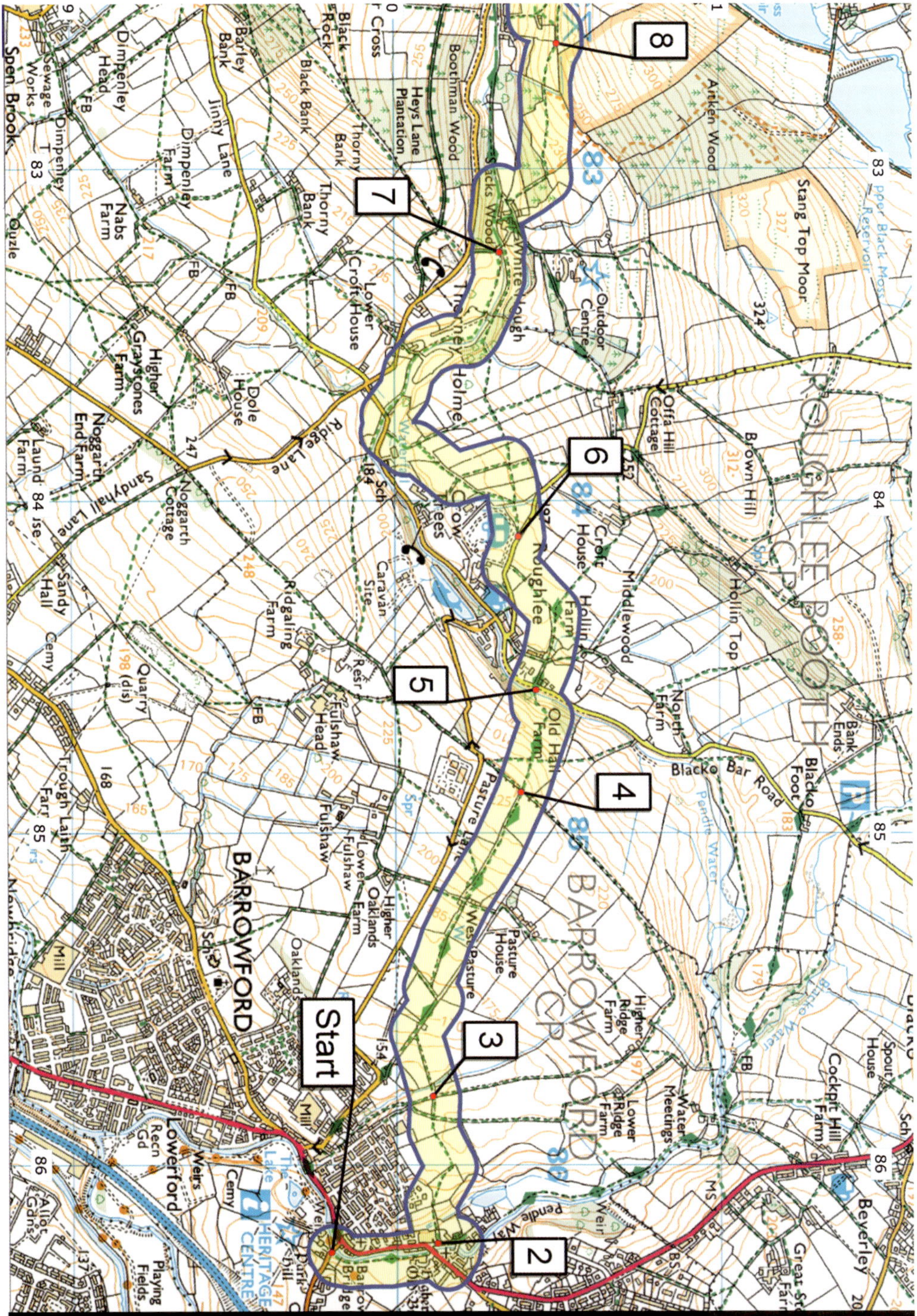
Start
2
3
4
5
6
7
8
BARROWFORD
BARROWFORD CP
ROUGHLEE BOOTH CP
Roughlee
Blacko Bar Road
Pasture Lane
Ridge Lane
Sandyhall Lane
Jinny Lane
Arken Wood
Stang Top Moor
Boothman Wood
Heys Lane Plantation
Whitehough
Outdoor Centre
Thorney Holme
Crow Trees
Caravan Site
Old Hall Farm
West Pasture
Pasture House
Higher Ridge Farm
Lower Ridge Farm
Water Meetings
Pendle Water
Lowerford
Heritage Centre

Barley to Rigg of England 3.7 Miles

9. Turn left onto the footpath, opposite the old chapel. Follow this enclosed path with stream on the right and then over a footbridge to enter a large field. Head diagonally left over this field to go through a gateway at the top far corner. Head gently uphill, with the fence line on your left, through several gates and stiles, to turn left at a farm building at SD 811402. Walk for about 270m to pick up a track nearer the reservoir. A ladder stile leads into a wooded area. Go steeply down through the trees and turn left to cross a stile at the bottom. Turn left to find a path on your right leading to cross over the stream.

10. Up the steps ahead into the wood. Continue steeply uphill into the trees, with the path bearing left after some 300m. This path then leaves the plantation, turning right onto a track. Follow this to cross a stile at the forest corner.

11. Turn left with a fence on your left. Go through a gate in a stone wall. Follow a wall on your left to another stile. Now downhill to reach a gate on the left SD820395. Do not go through the gate, but bear right across open ground slightly east of south east, using a way-marker post to reach a path downhill into Newchurch-in-Pendle. Pass the Church (worth a look) on the left and bear right at the next junction, on Well Head Road, to the disused (Faughs) quarry on the right, then follow the track on the left toward Rigg of England.

12. Through the farmyard, bear right and then turn right on the track for 25m, to use a metal kissing gate. Go diagonally across the field to cross a stile in a fence, continuing in the same direction to cross a footbridge.

Faughs Quarry from Rigg of England (Ian T-B)

13. Follow the path to Bull Hole, then turn left past Tinedale Farm, up the hill toward the road, but turn hard right just before you cross the stile.

8

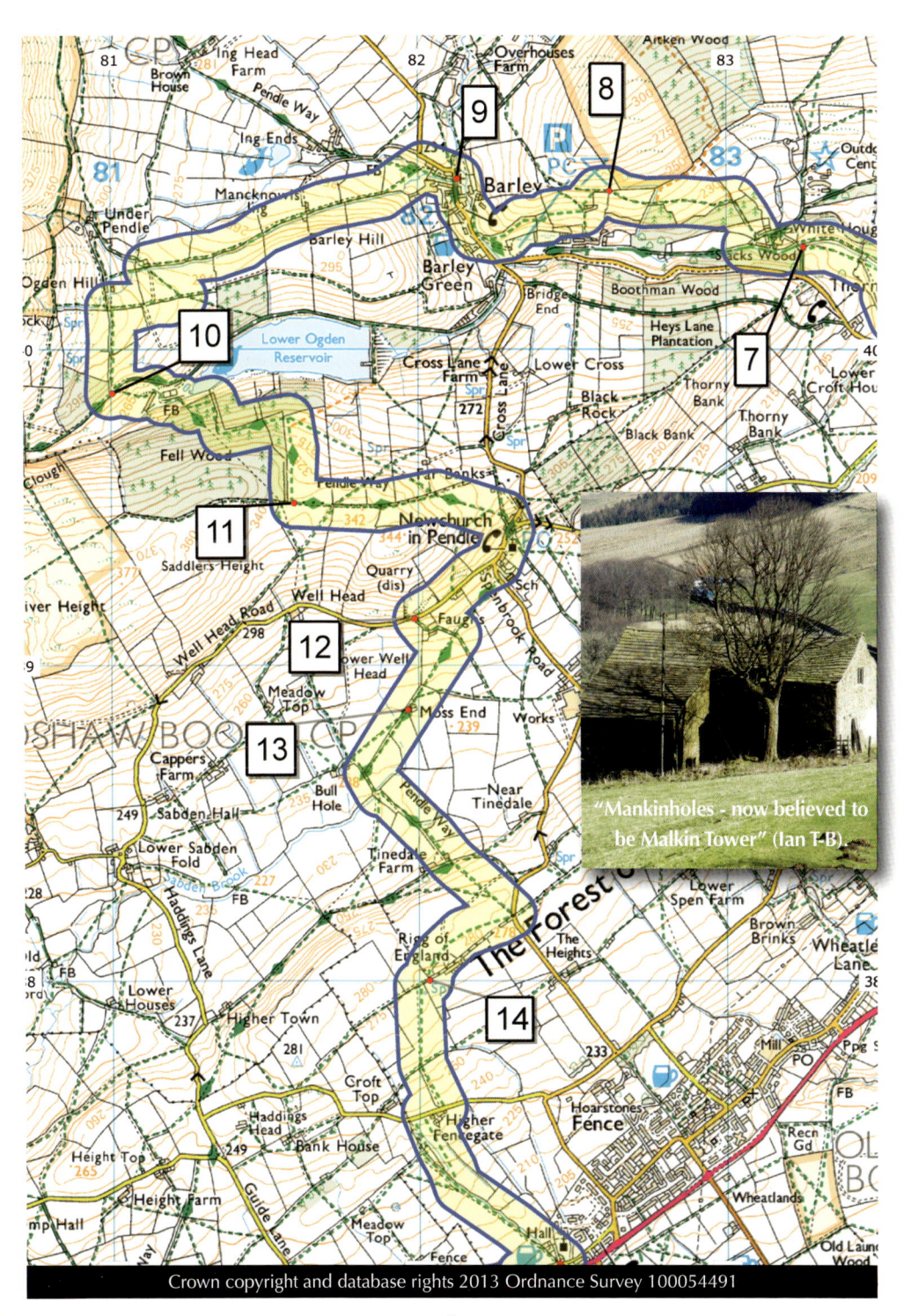

"Mankinholes - now believed to be Malkin Tower" (Ian T-B).

Rigg of England to Higham 2 Miles

14. Track past Rigg of England Farmhouse on your left, using a wooden gate, then an old steel kissing gate. Head slightly right of downhill, to cross a small footbridge, then bear slightly left to aim for a gate entering a lane. Turn right, then left, through a narrow stone stile into a ménage and head downhill over a couple of stiles, the second of which holds a way-marker bearing right, to use a gate. Cross the stream and bear left downhill along the stream/hedge, past a fine Scout Hut, to a lane. Turn right and follow the lane to the A6068 and cross very carefully.

15. Turn right towards Higham on the pavement, passing Ashlar House (which is private, please don't disturb) to reach Lower White Lee Farm. Turn left into the yard past the main house and find a marked footpath through a barn. Use the track exit past a steel gate into a field and follow the field edge on your right to cross the next stile. Follow the track, bearing half left across open ground, to find a stile and cross stream in woods and up the bank on the far side. Continue with the hedge on the right for 200m then bear left to pass behind a barn at Heys to find a ladder stile.

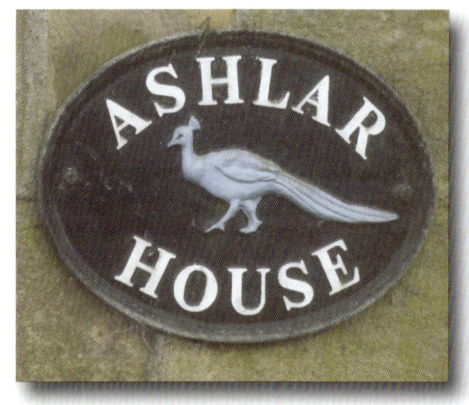

16. Cross the field passing to the left of the fenced-in farm buildings to traverse a lane via a gate. Over the stile opposite and go diagonally right across the field towards the church steeple at Higham. Exit onto the A 6068 road and turn left on the road for 50 m. Negotiate the road with great care to a gap into an enclosed path. Follow the path into Higham and turn left.

Ashlar House

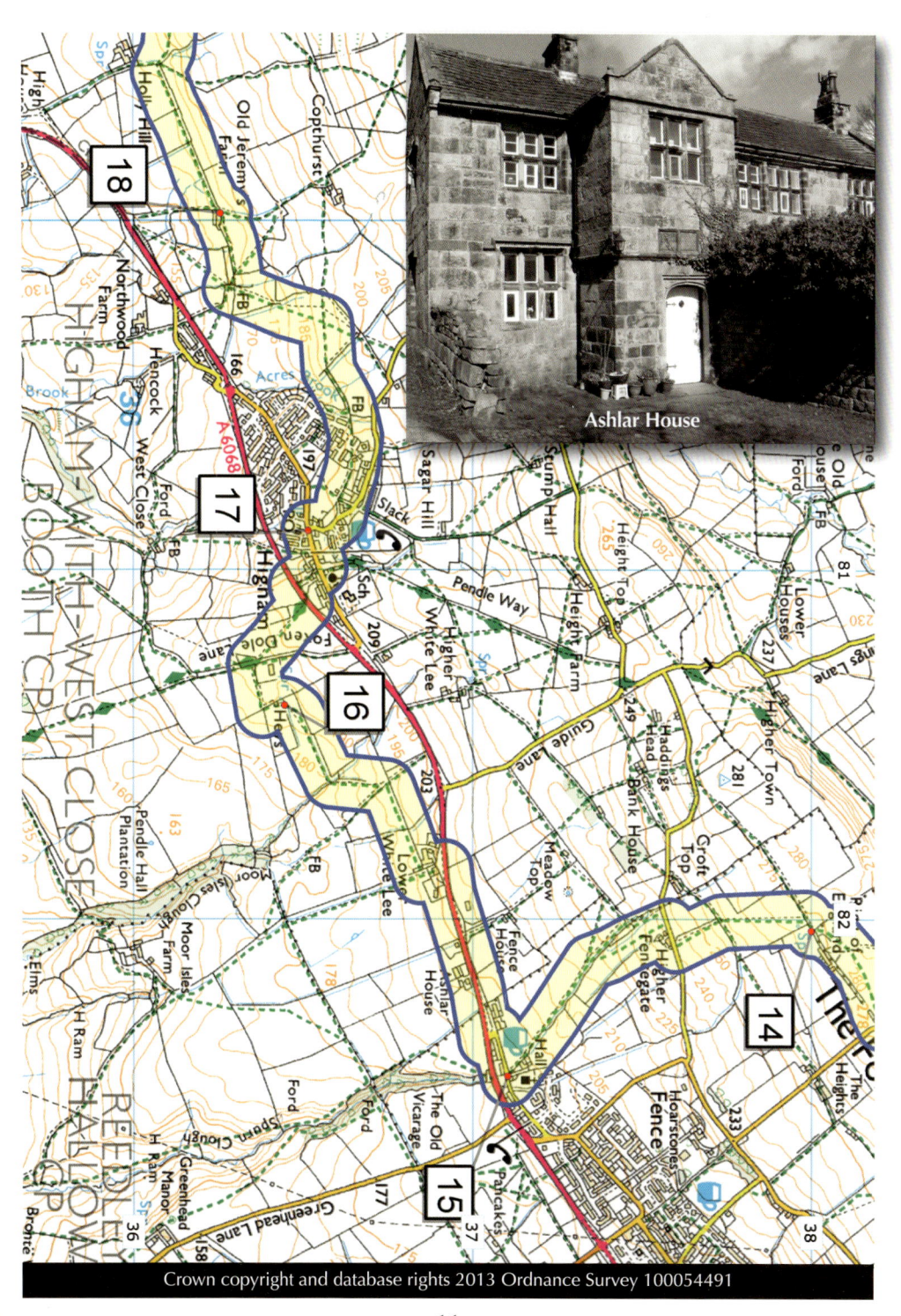

Higham to Law Farm 3.6 miles

17. At the 4 Alls Inn turn right up Sabden Road, taking the first left (Croft Lane) and follow the footpath between the houses and across the playing field. Follow on the footpath to turn right at the electricity substation on your right and cross the footbridge. Keep on the footpath passing the next field boundary, turn left when another footpath crosses yours, turning south.

18. Through the steel gate in the far corner of that field and continue on the same line, soon turning right to pick up a near-hidden stile and then turn left toward a wooden gate. Take the path across a footbridge, and bear left then right, behind Old Jeremy's Farm. Continue in the same direction with the hedge on your right, until your reach another footbridge. Carry on in the same general direction, threading between the farmhouse and barn, down their drive to another Sabden Road, which is crossed with care at Height Side.

4 Alls Inn - In the time of the witches, this was a "Leet" court

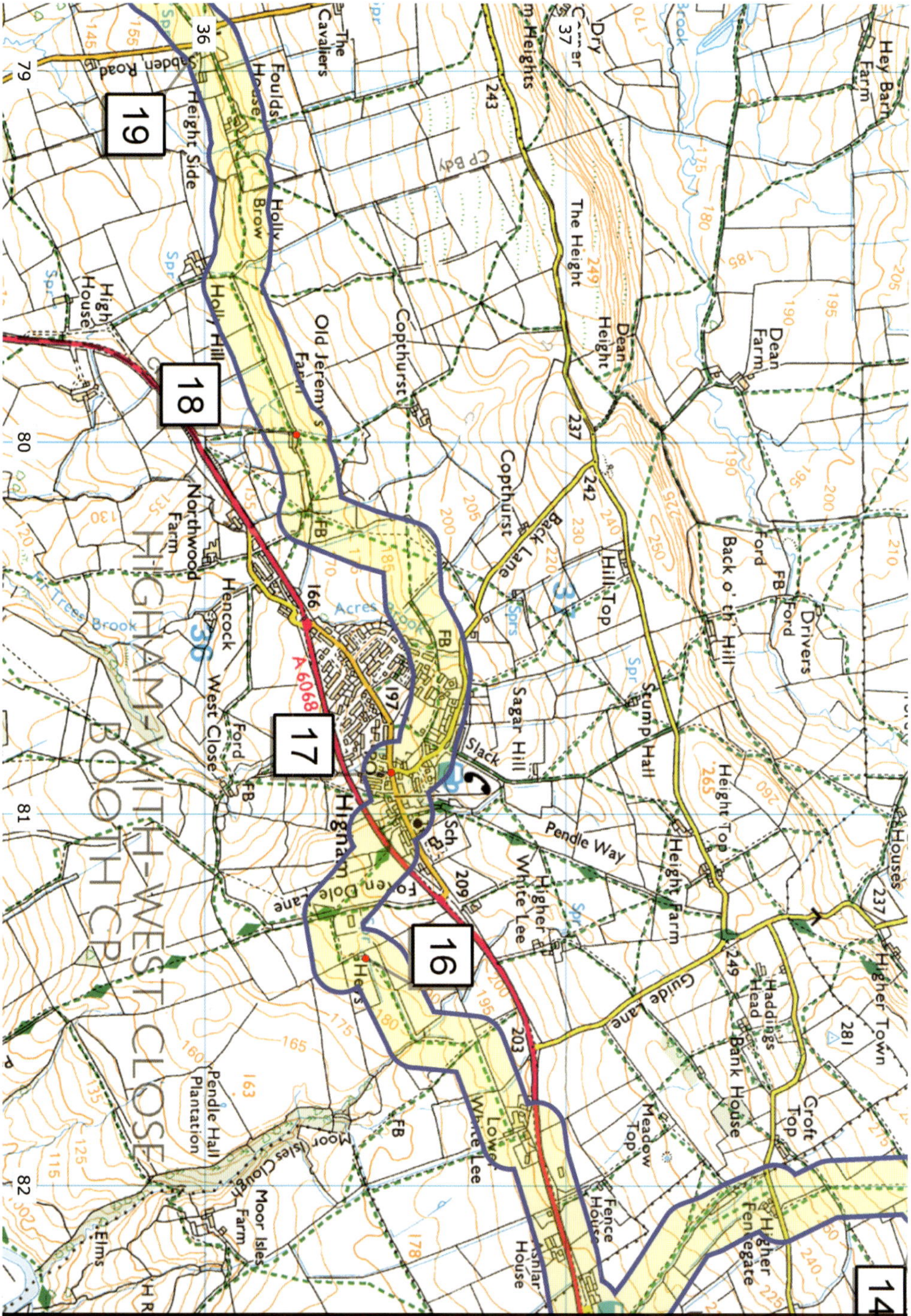
19
18
17
16
14
Sabden Road
Height Side
Foulds House
The Cavaliers
Holly Brow
Holly Hill
High House
Old Jeremy's Farm
Copthurst
The Height
Dean Height
Dean Farm
Back Lane
Hill Top
Back o' th' Hill
Drivers Ford
Sagar Hill
Stump Hall
Slack
Height Top
Pendle Way
Higher White Lee
Height Farm
Guide Lane
Haddings Head
Higher Town
Bank House
Croft Top
Meadow Top
Fence House
Higher Fence Gate
Ashlar House
Lower White Lee
Fir Trees Brook
Acres Brook
Northwood Farm
Hencock
West Close
Ford
Higham
Sch
A 6068
HIGHAM-WITH-WEST CLOSE BOOTH CP
Pendle Hall Plantation
Moor Isles Clough
Moor Isles Farm
Elms
CP Bdy

Law Farm to Read Old Bridge 2 miles

19. Continue the same direction, through Priddy Bank Farm and the wood behind, until you reach a metalled track turning left toward a double steel gate, then through a steel kissing-gate through a wood, and resume your previous direction. Cross the field, though the gate and across the next field to the bottom left-hand corner, where you come out on to Trapp Lane, opposite Law Farm.

20. Turn left along the lane. Cross the stile next to a red gate on your right, go up the rise, over the stile and keep on, behind the houses, until you reach an unusual concrete stile taking you onto Whins Lane. Follow that lane through the edge of the village, passing the top of George Lane, until you come to Hammond Lane leading off to your left. Follow it around the back of Read Hall until you emerge from the woods, then turn right and follow another track around the edge of the woodland, across the park, until you emerge through a steel gate, in a pleasant lay-by near to Read Old Bridge

Read Old Bridge was the site of a Civil War battle in April 1643. A group of local Roundheads ambushed and beat the Lancashire Royalist Army here.

© John Sparshatt 2013

Huntroyde Wood
© John Sparshatt 2013

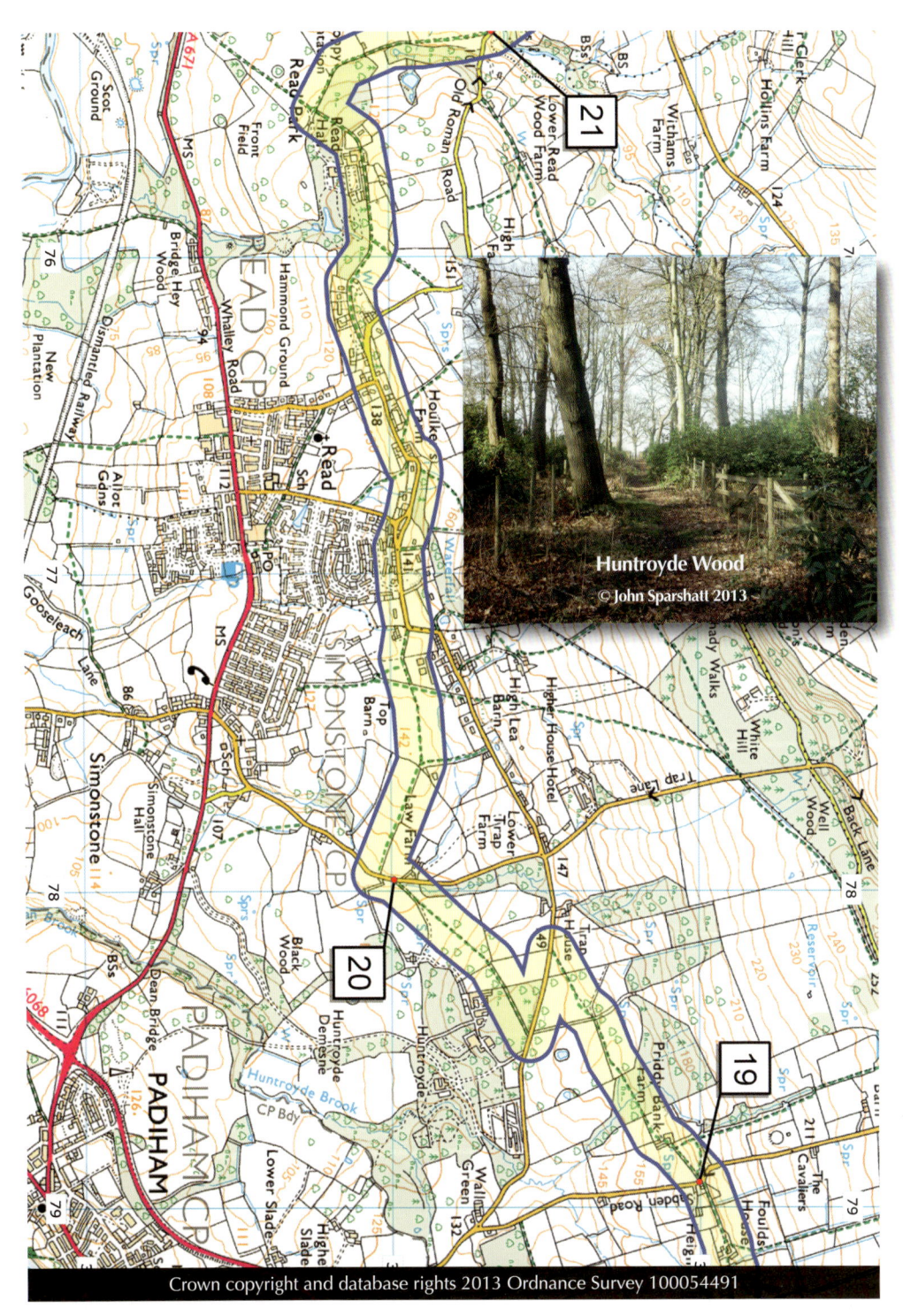

Crown copyright and database rights 2013 Ordnance Survey 100054491

Read Old Bridge to Clitheroe 4.9 miles

21. Cross Read Old Bridge and use the track on the left toward Easterley Farm. Turn right at the stile, toward Portfield. Use the stile under the signpost and turn right. Turn left at the road junction, following the sign marked "Cul-de-Sac". Pass the golf club entrance and take the footpath on your left, swinging right and gently uphill about halfway across Clerk Hill field. Use either the gate or the stile at the top, followed by another stile, where you turn left. Keep going north through Deer Park Wood. Keep north until you emerge on a lane threading between Sheep Cote and Wiswell Hall Farms.

22. Follow the lane down to the post box, turning right along Pendleton Road and left at the Old School/War Memorial, into Back Lane (signposted "Barrow"). Follow this for about 50m and bear right at Greenacres (painted white!) along the track, which is a 13^{th}C road! Use this path through several fields, keeping right of the power lines, crossing the bridges and last field diagonally toward a gate to the A59. Using the grass track set back from the road, walk to the far end of the lay-by. Then cross the A59, remembering that some drivers do stick to the 60 mph limit, and find the stile into a field, which you cross diagonally to a gate. Then cross the next field to the stile about 20m past a field-gate, into Clitheroe Road.

Approaching Wiswell from Deer Park Wood
Ancient sunken path into Wiswell
© John Sparshatt 2013

16

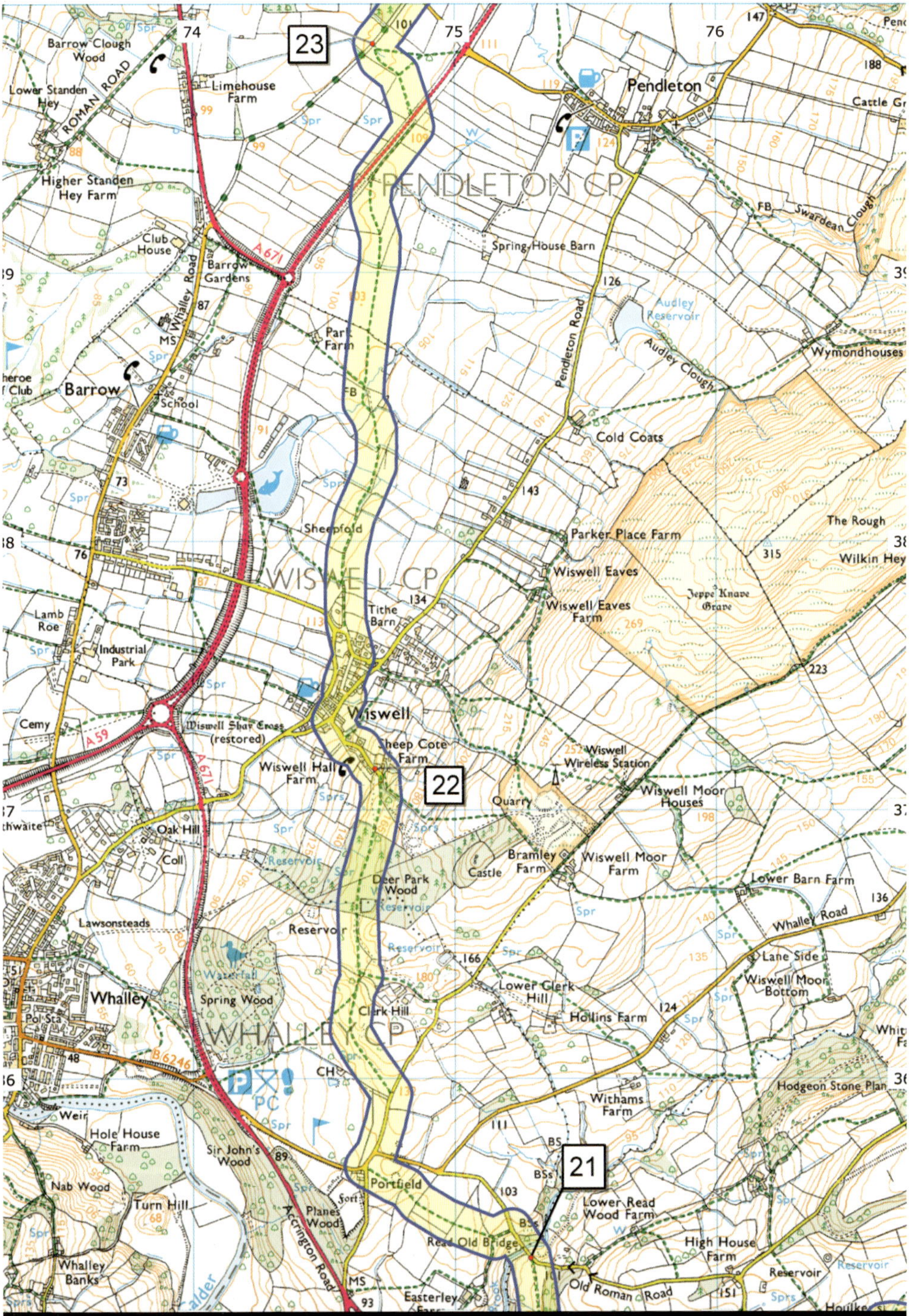
23
22
21
74
75
76
Barrow Clough Wood
Lower Standen Hey
ROMAN ROAD
Limehouse Farm
Pendleton
Cattle Gr
Higher Standen Hey Farm
PENDLETON CP
Swardean Clough
Club House
Barrow Gardens
A671
Spring House Barn
Whalley Road
Park Farm
Audley Reservoir
Audley Clough
Pendleton Road
Wymondhouses
Barrow
School
Cold Coats
Sheepfold
Parker Place Farm
The Rough
Wilkin Hey
Wiswell Eaves
Wiswell Eaves Farm
Jeppe Knave Grave
WISWELL CP
Tithe Barn
Lamb Roe
Industrial Park
Cemy
A59
Wiswell
Wiswell Shay Cross (restored)
Sheep Cote Farm
Wiswell Hall Farm
Wiswell Wireless Station
Quarry
Wiswell Moor Houses
Oak Hill
Coll
Reservoir
Castle
Bramley Farm
Wiswell Moor Farm
Deer Park Wood
Lower Barn Farm
Lawsonsteads
Whalley Road
Lane Side
Wiswell Moor Bottom
Lower Clerk Hill
Whalley
Spring Wood
Waterfall
Clerk Hill
Hollins Farm
WHALLEY CP
B6246
Hodgeon Stone Plan
Withams Farm
Weir
Hole House Farm
Sir John's Wood
Portfield
Nab Wood
Turn Hill
Planes Wood
Accrington Road
Lower Read Wood Farm
Read Old Bridge
High House Farm
Whalley Banks
Easterley
Old Roman Road
Reservoir

Clitheroe to Hancocks Farm 3.0 miles

23. Turn right to walk on for about 250m, turning left along the side wall of Standen Hall, and go across the back and cross a footbridge to school playing fields, which are skirted left and then right. Turn right along Langshaw Drive, but almost immediately left along a marked footpath to Longmoor Rd. Turn right to Turner St. and then left to Queen's Road, past the school.

24. Turn left into Queensway (the Inner Bypass). Use the Pelican crossing carefully and turn right to the far end of Homebase. Turn left and go over Wilkin Bridge, past an old Chapel (now the Muslim Centre) and straight across Lowergate, up the narrow stone steps, turning right along Moor Lane.

25. Go through Castlegate, Castle St and Market St, to Church Brow, and then the Parish Church grounds. Zigzag though the churchyard to Brennand St and then follow it to Railway View Road, then turn right and left into Waddington Road. Follow the road on, straight over Brungerley Bridge. Walk about ¼ mile on from the bridge, almost opposite Waddow Hall, and follow a footpath fingerpost off to the right, towards Lillands, and go onward toward Waddington School.

Former Zion Church, Lowergate, Clitheroe
© Copyright John Sparshatt

Clitheroe Castle

19

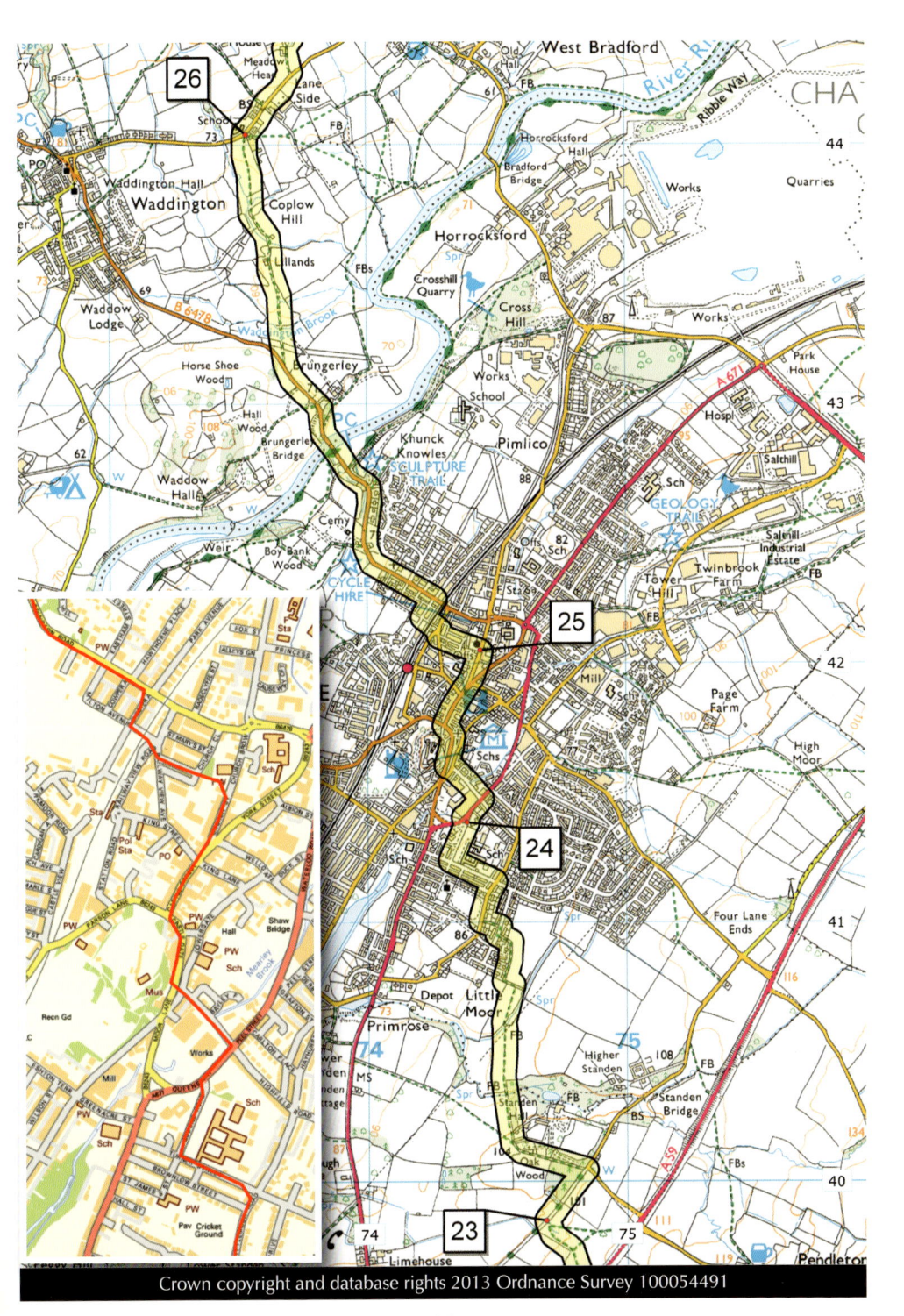

Hancocks Farm to Fell Side 3.7 miles

26. Turn right along Waddington Road and then turn left up the second footpath, toward and heading north, to Meadow Head on your left. Over the stile on your right, bearing diagonally right to the far corner of the field, over a well-nettled stile (or through the field-gate) at the stream, turning north-west, toward and past Owl Cottage on your right, over two stiles. Bear half-left around another building and go over another stile by a steel field-gate. Cross two fields, using the tram-lines if there are standing crops, aiming between a house and a bungalow, over another stile and through a steel garden gate. Continue, turning right through the buildings, on about 100m to Dove Syke Nursery, then picking up the FP almost hidden on your left, and head diagonally across the field, toward the end of the trees. Cross the stile and small bridge and go north again, emerging on Moor Lane by Hancocks Farm.

27. Turn left up Moor Lane, starting as tarmac, but deteriorating, through being: metalled; soft soil; and then turf, for just over 1 mile, through a right/left joggle.

28. By a couple of old stone gate posts the track turns right, toward the forestry area. At those woods, turn left through the gates, again on a defined track. Take the "right" choice at the first and second footpath junctions, crossing an open area toward and over a wooden ladder stile over a stone wall.

29. The footpath continues steadily westward across Far Brown Hill, comprising a pair of wheel ruts with turf between. At a junction it then suddenly turns hard right in a north-east direction. Again, follow this track across the grouse moor, as it gradually swings north and descends along a well-defined track. After that, it's easy to navigate northward, along the track and down to Fell Side.

Tagglesmire
©John Sparshatt 2012

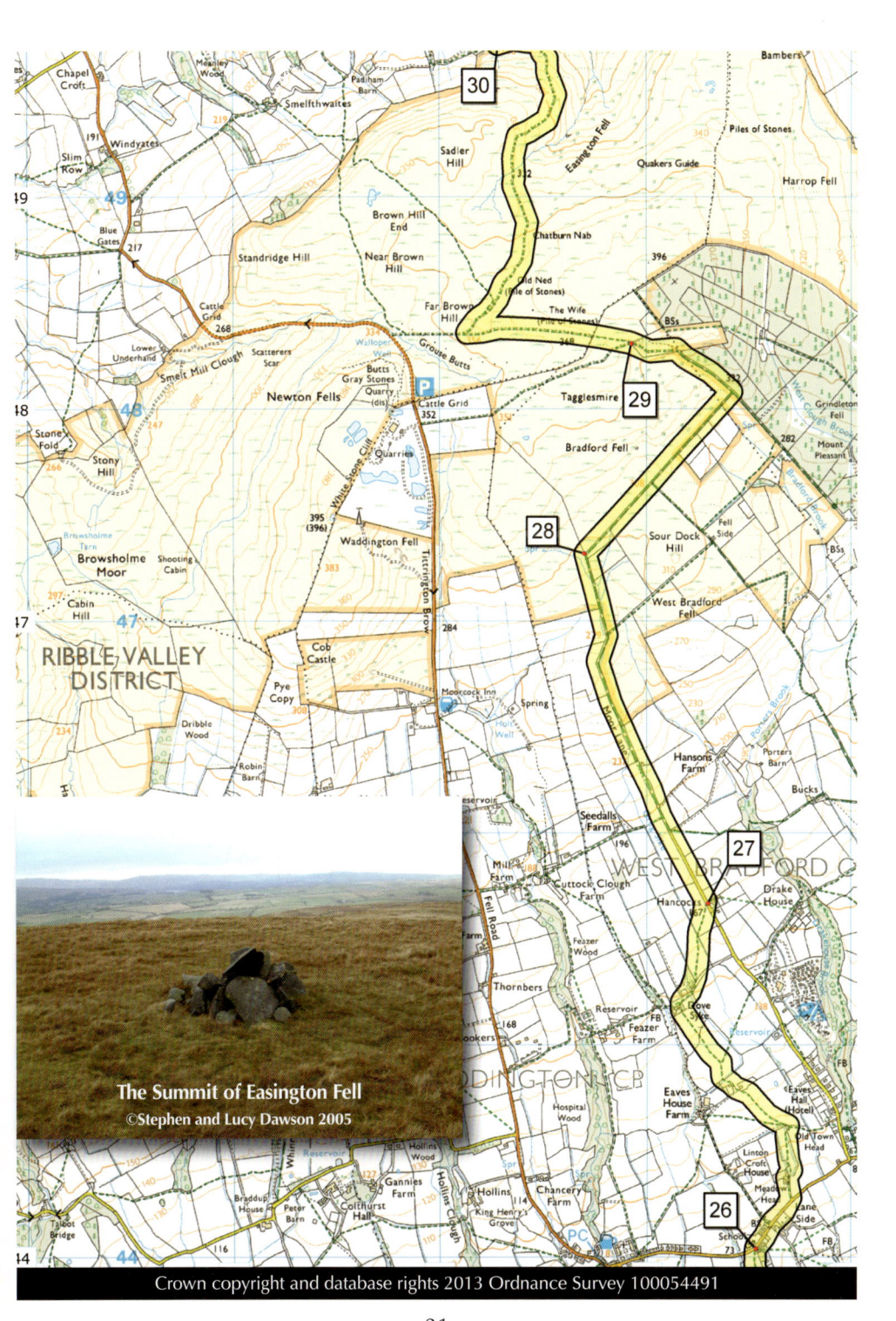

The Summit of Easington Fell
©Stephen and Lucy Dawson 2005

Crown copyright and database rights 2013 Ordnance Survey 100054491

21

Fell Side to Slaidburn 2.1 miles

30. Go on to Skelshaw and over the footbridge. As you go on down to Broadhead Farm and, once past Gaughey Hill, you will start to see Slaidburn. It's safest to turn right up the hill and then follow the marked path on your left, rather than risk traffic on the blind hairpin bend on the downhill road. Continue through the village, past the car park/bus stop and War Memorial and, opposite the Hark to Bounty Inn, find the YHA (01200 446656) and village shop on your left.

Slaidburn to Lanshaw 1.3 miles

31. This and the next are the easiest pieces of navigation, but remote. Walk northwest, along Town End, with the Hark to Bounty Inn on your right, until you come to the NHS Health Centre. A few m beyond, you will see a timber kissing gate on your right. Take this through the wood and over the ladder stile and then through two gates.

32. Follow the hedge/fence on your left and cross another ladder stile, then cross the stile on your right and cross a small footbridge. Cross the field diagonally left to right, to a field gate. Follow the hedge on your right and you will suddenly find a grassy lane turning right, leading into a farmyard.

33. Cross the yard, with the old craft shop on your right and a barn on your left, and bear left onto a track. A little over 100m along the track you will take a footpath off to your right, opposite a barn. Take this, across the farm track, to the far corner and continue onward. Cross the brook on the same line, heading for the near side of the barn, where you can turn right along a lane. After about ¾ mile, at the top of this lane, you will come to a gate, intended to keep vehicular traffic off the Roman Road.

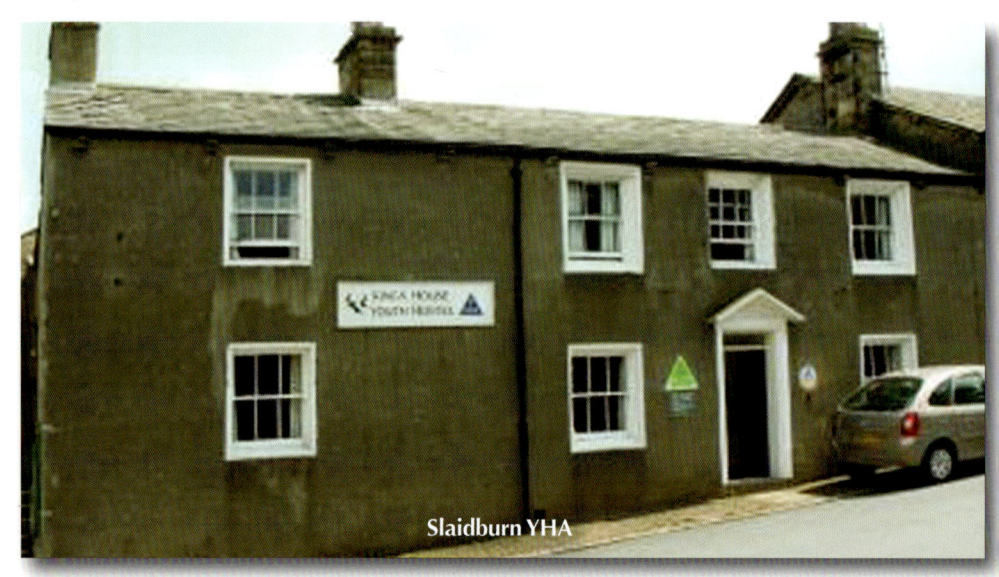

Slaidburn YHA

Slaidburn Bridge

Brennands Endowed School, Slaidburn

Crown copyright and database rights 2013 Ordnance Survey 100054491

© Christine Seddon 2013

Lanshaw to High Salter 8.6 Miles

34. Turn right and follow the rough gated road, which becomes Hornby Road when it crosses the Lancaster City boundary, for about 9 miles. You are crossing Salter Fell. On a reasonably clear day you should be able to see, from parts of it: The Three Peaks of Yorkshire; The Howgills; the Southern Lakeland Hills; Pendle Hill; Morcambe Bay; Heysham Power Station; and Lancaster City.

© Christine Seddon 2013

Crown copyright and database rights 2013 Ordnance Survey 100054491

25

High Salter to Deep Clough 2.3 miles

35. At High Salter, leave the Hornby Road as you pass through a field gate on your left, just before the buildings, and pick up the waymarked path. Skirt round barns which are on your right, then follow the right-hand field boundary downhill. Cross over the wooden stile, onto a track, and turn left to Mallowdale Bridge and then steeply up again toward Mallowdale Farm. Take the wooden stile on the right before the farm. Walk in front of a 'garden' wall, and bear leftish down the field. Locate a track and stile descending toward a small stream with a footbridge. Cross and follow wooden steps up the far bank.

36. Walk diagonally to your right, up the field, with the fence line on your right, and climb to a stone stile. Follow the wall on your left up the field to a field gate. Bear right across this field, to a gate before Haylot Farm. Walk to the right on the track, in front of the farmhouse, to another gate. Cross the farm road and bear left to wooden stile to the left of a field gate. Continue, with a fence on your left, down to another wooden stile. Go uphill, rightish, in a westerly direction to reach a stile in a section of stone wall. Once over this, continue uphill, bearing slightly right, ignoring the path coming in from your right, then bear left over a stream to reach a gate, then go through another on the right. Walk along, with the fence line on your left, and go left and right through the gate before a barn. Cross the field to a gateway into Deep Clough.
There are 6- and 8-bedded accommodation units available here, self-catering, as well as selling organic rare-breed beef, lamb and pork *(01524770574/07984877164 carole@deepclough.co.uk).* If you are not stopping overnight, walk up the farm track to the small but good Roeburndale Road, to meet your transport.

37. Assuming that you did stay at Deep Clough, walk up the stone track to Roeburndale Road and turn right to the next cattle grid. Immediately after the cattle grid, turn left onto the rough surfaced track, which is a concessionary bridleway. Follow it, with the wall on your left, for about 1¼ miles, turning left at the end, onto a metalled road.

Mallendale Farm, Summer 2005
©Tarja Wilson 2005

Gallows Hill, Mallendale
©Tarja Wilson 2004

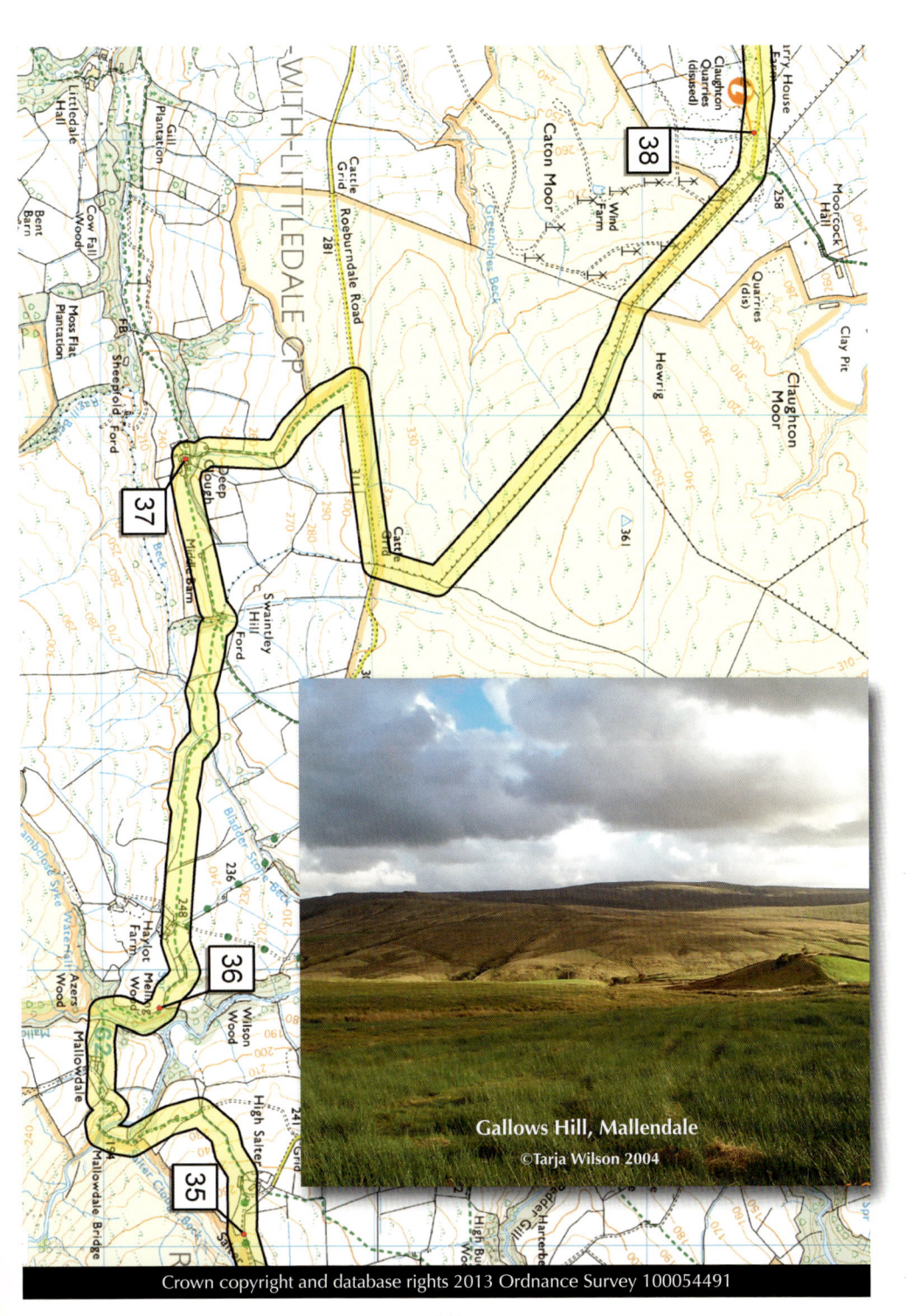

Crown copyright and database rights 2013 Ordnance Survey 100054491

27

Deep Clough to Crook O'Lune 5.7 miles

38. *At the point marked for Tourist Information there are picnic benches, which might serve for a morning break.* Follow the unclassified Quarry Road down to Moorside Farm, and turn right down Moor Lane, past the school. After going over the bridge, turn right. In front of the Black Bull pub, cross the fairly busy road and enter Holme Lane. Ignore the footpath sign to your left and continue to the A683.

39. Cross that road into a lane directly opposite. Almost immediately, turn left onto the Lune Valley Ramble, which is a multi-use route, converted from an old rail track. Along here, in summer, is a car park at the Crook O' Lune, with a bikers' café *(Woodies, open July-August, Wed-Sun, rest of year Fri-Sun, 0900-1500)* toilets and picnic tables with a nice view.

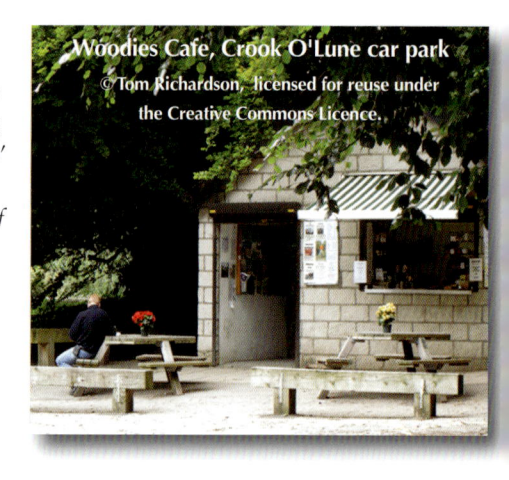

Woodies Cafe, Crook O'Lune car park
©Tom Richardson, licensed for reuse under the Creative Commons Licence.

Crook o'Lune view, upstream
the view from the picnic benches

29

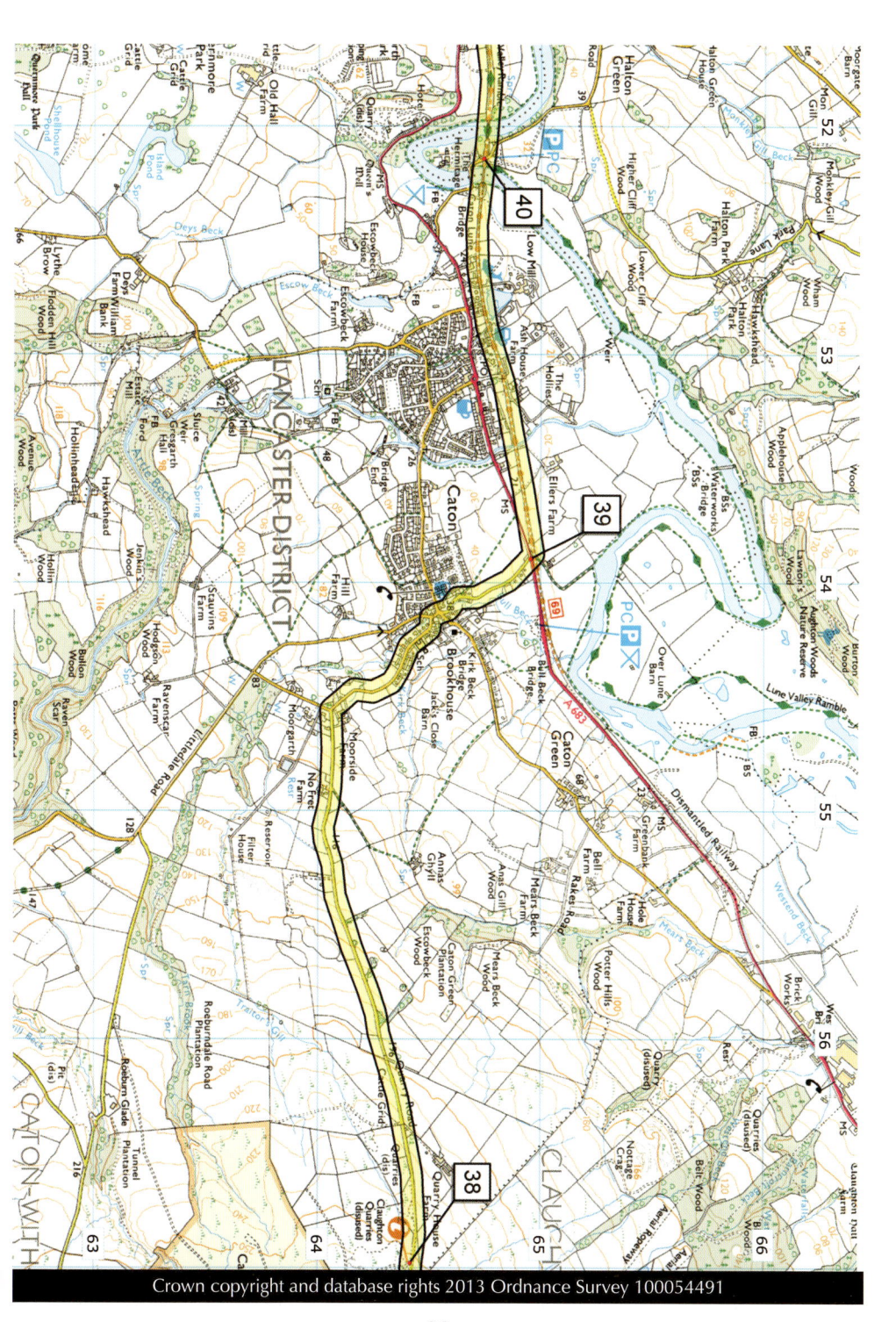

Crook O'Lune to Lancaster Castle 4.9 miles

40. Continue on this track for another 1¼ miles, until after passing an old station, to Denny Beck, which is just downstream of a weir. Turn left to Denny Beck Lane and follow its wriggles up to the A683 again and cross, just as carefully, straight into Grimeshaw Lane, which is subject to a Definitive Map Modification Order that should make it into a BOAT or RUPP in the very near future!

41. Follow the lane south for 1 mile to cross the M6. Take the bridleway to your left, which is, for a change, called Moor Lane. The modern and massive set of buildings on your right is Lancaster Farms Young Offenders Institution.

42. Then, the much older and massive set of red stone buildings to your left is Lancaster Moor Hospital, an asylum that was started in June 1816 and closed in December 1999. To your right is a sizable cemetery. Moor Lane becomes Stone Row Head for about 200 m. Then turn right onto Quernmore Road for another 200m and cross over near the mini-roundabout.

43. Turn left down Parkgate Drive and then almost immediately up a grassy slope to a black-painted steel kissing gate. Follow the path on your left and then take the first fork to the right up a slope. Continuing up this direction you will soon come to a massive set of black-painted steel gates. Bear left through these, toward the impressive Ashton Memorial. Pass it on the right hand side, down the slope and through an old quarry area and onward to Wyresdale Road. Somewhere in this area was Gallows Lane, where the witches were hung, now disappeared.

44. Turn right, and head down into Lancaster City centre. As you cross another main road you will find you are now on Moor Gate and, after bending slightly left, at the next crossroads and the canal bridge, it becomes Moor Lane! On the right hand side of Moor Lane, at the junction with Brewery Lane, is the Golden Lion pub at which, according to the green Civic Society plaque, the Witches were offered a last drink on their way to the gallows. The road widens at Stone Well. Cross over the main one-way road and bear right, to continuing in the same direction up Church Street to the Judges' Lodgings (now a very interesting museum) bearing left and then right to the entrance to Lancaster Castle, The prison was closed, by the Ministry of Justice, on economic grounds, in March 2011.
The Crown Court was relocated in June 2014, so a full tour of the courts, museum and dungeons is now strongly recommended.
(01524 64998; lancastercastle@lancashire.gov.uk).

John O'Gaunt Gateway, Lancaster Castle

31

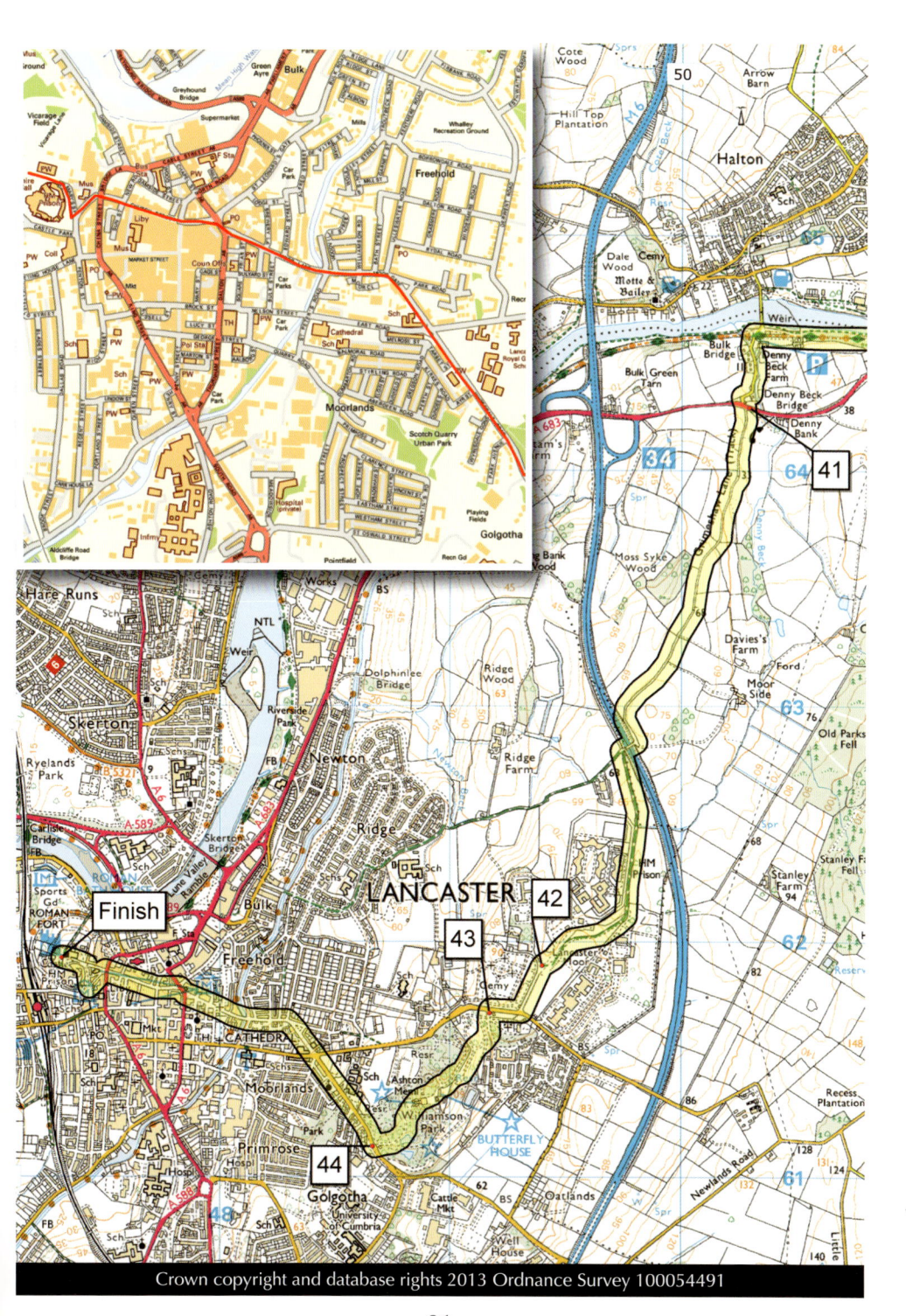

Acknowledgements

This walk and book could not have been developed without the work of a lot of people:

- The original concept came from Sue and Pete Flowers of Green Close Studios, Melling, who also managed development of almost all the artistic outcomes of the project. They persuaded our present Poet Laureate, Carol Anne Duffy, to write the poem for the walk, now embossed on ten cast-iron tercets, mostly set near the walk route, and entitled The Lancashire Witches. The irony of this fact is that the witches were executed as a scheme to curry favour with the then King, James 1st of England, the same king who first created the role of Sovereign's Poet Laureate.

- Tarja Wilson of Lancashire CC Environmental Community cheerfully gave much key strategic advice on possible issues along the route, which has proved informative, invaluable and encouraging.

- John Clayton's excellent *The Pendle Witch Fourth Centenary Handbook*, along with his freely-given advice, was used as the key source of current opinion of the key locations for the witches, and the most likely route they followed to Lancaster.

- Brian Jones, Chair of Lancaster Ramblers, persuaded Joy Greenwood, Pam Gorham, Lois Loudon and David and Val Johnson, all of Lancaster Ramblers, to contribute and advise on much valuable detail on the northern part of the route.
Likewise, John Lofthouse, Derek Seed and Phillip Proctor of Burnley Ramblers pioneered the early versions of the text from Barrowford, and survived.

- Ian Thornton-Bryar, a local Rambler, and John Sparshatt, Chair, the LDWA, developed the route and wrote and edited (several times!) most of the copy of this book.
Ian publishes as "Postmark Books, 71 Waddington Road, Clitheroe BB7 2HN. Telephone 01200 444829, e-mail: iant-b@talktalk.net".

- Produced by Bowland Graphics: 01200 447060
e-mail: info@bowlandgraphics.com

Advice to walkers:

This is a sustainable 51-mile long-distance walk that is very varied in the type of countryside along its route. Lovely wooded valleys contrast with high and really wild moorland fells and a couple of small historic urban areas – often giving magnificent views, are its main features. Don't be fooled by its pleasant walking – it can be wild in bad weather. Please, don't walk it alone - or at the very least inform someone exactly where you are and how they will know you have arrived – about 40% of the route has very poor or zero mobile (cell-phone) signal. Otherwise, no-one may know if you get into trouble. The local farmers can be very welcoming.
Please reciprocate, by following the Country Code in an exemplary fashion.